ISBN-13:
978-0963715210 (Magnetar Intertainment Enterprises)

ISBN-10:
0963715216

Printed in the U.S.A. for Worldwide Distribution

First Printing: 1992

Second Printing: 2012

DEDICATED...

to appreciation and application of Universal Living-Spirit, Infinite Intelligence and Power.

Content

Title	Page
The Future of the Moment's......	7
Mining Your African Diamond Mind......	8
Jazzyimandias......	10
The Awakening......	12
Love......	13
Undergrowth......	17
Grace Under Design......	18
To Sow The Fallow Ground......	20
In Praise of Living —LIFE......	21
To Dance in the SERENGETI Rains.....	23
As LIFE Lives......	24
Affirmations in the Law of Personal Growth......	31
The Ethos of Equinox......	34
The Nature of Friendship......	36
Self-Encounters Of The First Kind......	38
Choice and consequences......	39
Freedom in Chains......	41
Signals......	42
A Troubling Rain......	43
Umoja......	44
In Tears Of Prayer......	45
Magnets And Mastery......	48
Thoughts Are Tools......	50
I Sojourn I......	55
Imani......	57

As Spirit Leads.............................. 56

Psalms 40.................................... 59

A Gift Of The Wind.......................... 61

At The Top Of The Truth.................. 63

Ujamaa....................................... 65

Time.. 67

To The Inner Woman........................ 68

Songs Of Spring............................. 69

The Eros Of Moonlight 71

Wisdom Of Faith............................ 72

Diligence..................................... 73

The Principal Prize.......................... 74

In Touch With The Infinite............... 78

Genesis....................................... 82

Diamind...................................... 83

At The Mouths Of Babes................. 89

Momma's Alms.............................. 90

See It Through............................... 92

In Deep Soil................................. 93

Beyond Freedom............................ 94

Posterity..................................... 95

By Bread Alone.............................. 97

The Precepts Of Ptah-Hotep............. 98

ACKNOWLEDGMENTS

To the influence and friendship of my mother, Maxine who showed me how and whom to trust.

To my wife and children; to all of my closet family and friends, I will love you always.

To all of my teachers and mentors over the years; you inspiration continues on.

The Precepts of PTAH_HOTEP
Horne, Charles F.; Ph.D.(1917) *The Sacred Books And Early Literature of The East*, Parke, Austin and Lipscomb, Inc. New York, London

The Future of the Moment

After the "DREAM"
And beyond
"ANY MEANS" where
does your future lie?

Is he in school or
out shooting
pool, playing the fool
by and by?
Is she standing on her feet or lying in the sheets
in the hands of a nasty high?
Where are your Martin, your Malcolm, and your Marcus?
Where is your Mary, your Martha, your Maybelle?
Are they in living color or was it all just a fable?

How many Martins have been shot in the street?
How many Mary's have been killed in their sleep?

They're dying in the arms of violence and crack.
Shall they fall even more before you find your way back?

Back to the Love of an unselfish act;
Back to the Light of a world before Crack.
Back to the ONE where nothing is slack;
Let us each send to our Prodigals and tell them
that! **By Living Hope**

Mining Your African Diamond Mind

In ancient Africa roamed vast numbers of the most savage beasts. Loaded with claws and girded with strength, stamina and daggers for teeth, danger stalked the earth. Lions, Mandrills, Tigers, Hyenas and Wild Dogs all natural born killers. Yet the Antelope had horns and could out run most. Rhinos had their horns, strength and size to survive. Wildebeest came in vast number and simply out produced the odds. But what did you have; what did you do?

How did you rise above such hazards and danger without great speed or size to survive and progress; because history and archeology confirm that you out performed them all! You built and sustained the foundation of modern civilization on the shores of the Nile for thousands of years. You developed the basis of Modern Medicine, Chemistry, Astronomy, Mathematics, Architecture and exported Culture and Art around the world. You healed the sick and helped the weak. You gave birth to Giants and Masters of Masters. You were the first Light of the World.

Now you are again faced with many hazards and danger. Many of your Sons and Daughters are disproportionately sick, incarcerated, undereducated, misrepresented, self-destructed and scattered to the four corners of the world.

Think. How will you again rise above such savage beast, crime and drug ridden streets, diabolical and sinister Minds who set the cause in motion?

Your personal and professional development, depend on your answer. You see, many forms of riches have been extracted from Africa. And, indeed she contains much wealth; such as oil, gold, diamonds, spices and herbs, rich archaeological digs and of course ancient kemetic Egypt.

Therefore, I submit for your most profound consideration this conclusion: The greatest form of wealth ever extracted from Africa is the brand of thought and character which overcame the elements and the beast to build the foundations of modern civilization. It is that which I venture to call the African Diamond Mind. It is that wealth of strength that you originally used and must continue to employ; though with modern skill and insight to survive and progress.

Jazzyimandias

Awake In a Dream

Jahbril: When the mind of the sovereignty spoke to you Trismegistus, what did he speak of this present age? **Hermes:** Have you not read the scriptures, Jahbril? Are you also deficient in understanding the hieroglyphs? Everywhere is the evidence plain that the Mind called human must live as life lives. **Jahbril:** Do you mean that life is a thing unto itself? **Hermes:** How could anything living in the universe have come into existence if it was not preexistent in Life itself? The term existence means that which has come into being. Anything that comes into being must come from something that precedes it. Does not the child preexist in the loins and proceeds from a living womb? **Jahbril:** This example makes the matter clear Trismegistus. **Hermes:** Evolution, Jahbril is the growing edge of Creation. Though many in your age have confused the relative order of these things do not limit your understanding. Progress in the irrational creature is bound by immutable natural laws. These manifest as instincts. These laws and principles generate a generic imposition of conditions throughout nature. When prey is scarce, predators are scarce. When habitat is altered, so is the inhabitant. This determines the form and experiences of irrational creatures. **Jahbril:** Do you mean to suggest thrice greatest one, which man is not subject to universal principle? **Hermes:** Silence! Breathe not this irreverence into the Ether. It is impious to think such a thing. Ascend the Scale in your thought and you shall see the Mind called Human is girded with many powers, faculties and forces. Among the first of these is a two edged sword called Choice. The manifestation of this power alone imposes great consequences on this age. **Jahbril:** Surely it must be so. **Hermes:** Your age is filled the minds that blindly follow their passion and pleasures without regard to the consequences. They are not only mastered by their own faculties and forces; but many other perturbations outside of their interest rule them. Are you surprised Jahbril that I said your faculties and forces bear rule over you? When your eyes ingest your desires wantonly, who is your master? When your thought is scattered and vain, who is your Master? When you imagination is undisciplined and habituated to folly, who is your Master? When your will is without reason, who is your Master? **Jahbril:** I believe it pious to expect my faculties and forces to serve my highest interest and life's purposes in me. **Hermes:** Well said my friend. **Jahbril:** This mastery you speak of explains many things of the scriptures and the mysteries Trismegistus. **Hermes:** Yes, but let this suffice for now; let us return to your question of this age. Does it not follow that when one moves a bowl of water, the water inside is moved along with the bowl? And does it not also follow that when the water contained inside the bowl moves in a contrary direction to the movement of the bowl it will be wasted out? **Jahbril:** This point is very clear. **Hermes:** The example is insufficient; but the principle is clear. When, he, who no name can contain, asserts choice and preference, all things moving in a contrary direction are brought to naught. Now it is written, and it is so Jahbril, that the mind called Man is created after the image and likeness of his Creator. Now I ask you, if this Creator is asserting his will in the direction of his choice and the created is asserting his will to the contrary, what did Poimandres say to me concerning this age in the growing edge of Creation? **Jahbril:** It is as it is written. Peace and power to you Trismegistus. All praise, glory and honor to the highest who is One and All, All and One.

The Awakening

One set his heart to seek relief
From the deep sleep;
So the sun was sent to the One
With this bright,
Celestial Light:
"From whence comes the Dawn,
And to whence goes the Dusk,
Whence is thy substance of hope;
Whence is thy Trust?"
Celestine dream
How you do sing
To the free and sleep alike!
Then One set his heart to know
The purpose of life, love and light;
And this he found to be most
Good and right:
"As life is to live,
So is love to give
And light is to reveal
The way of Truth
to the sunlit hills of heaven."

LOVE

"To make Love like the Bee makes her Honey is deep; to fake Love, like the Thief makes his money is cheap"©-- Author. I have for some time now desired to write a short essay on the subject of Love. By disclaimer, I consider myself a Poet and Naturalist, with Scientific to Analytical tendencies. Therefore, my treatment of the subject reflects that point of view. I think that Love is indeed a splendid Thing and an amazing Word, with many uses. This suggests that we need some definition for context. This is the purpose of my Essay. Notwithstanding Webster's collegiate definition; LOVE, as it appears to me, is so much more than the Word(s) that we use to express it.

In fact, most of us experience Love as an expression of various degrees of Emotion. By degrees, I mean similar to the degrees of temperature on a Thermostat. For instance, we might find ourselves saying "I love French Vanilla Ice Cream" or "I love your Hair Style". This is a very different expression than saying to a Lover, "I Love You"; which might be a very different expression yet then saying to another "I'm In Love with you". Similarly, saying "I Love my Dog" is a very different degree of expression then saying "I love my Daughter". So, if we imagine a scale of the degrees of Love; we'll find that it has a very wide range from which to determine our "Temperature".

Following this train of thought, one might easily see that the word Love has multiple meanings and an infinite possibility of degrees. When I reflect on the expression "To Make Love", I'm caught in the idea that two or more people can bake Love as if it were a Cake? If this is true then with the correct ingredients, in the correct sequence and timing; do we actually create the Emotion? Or perhaps might this be something different in kind all together, like sexual satisfaction disguising itself as Love? I'm not entirely sure myself.

Nonetheless, I do believe that when two people are filled with *genuine emotions of deep care and concern for one another, passion, commitment, mutual trust & respect, with loving kindness come together as one physical being in perfect harmony*; these are in fact the essential ingredients for "making love". Such an influx of these ingredients has the distinct possibility to infuse a Baby with the Love of its Parents. "This is the kind of Love that will grow a Tree" — Author

So I would focus my thoughts, my emotion on the object that the word is referring to. I chose to believe that as the great Playwright, William Shakespeare so truly wrote "A Rose by any other name would still smell as sweet". The higher degrees of the Emotion of Love have its own origins; its own beginnings; its own place in the Life-Principle. It doesn't matter whether we speak of it in English, Spanish, German or the "language of Love", French; Love is what it is because it IS!

So, with this in mind, I asked a French friend of mine her thoughts on the subject:

> "*Speak to me of Love Francis*; that I might know its spirit and kin." I whispered in the dark. "*Love is, my Love*", she murmured back "*the kiss of a beautiful butterfly to the lilies of the field. She is the gentle touch of rain on the orchards of summer. The Wind and Waves are of her the offspring between Sun and Moon. Her true name is yet unknown to Men; but by her many children, she is wonderful to behold in deed. Her essence is light in the eyes of*

*innocence, a suckling gaze up from the milk of life. Hers is the hope that springs eternal; the **purpose of Life in You**. "*

*"But, how will I know that she's real and not a fantasy of my dreams? How will I know that she is not the cruel lies of hateful deceit? Is this not the way of her evil twin sister?" I questioned. "What you have heard" she purred, "is nothing more than myth and lore. Love is all there is and there is nothing else. She is as the Heat to the idea of Cold; cold is simply the absence of Heat. She is the feeling you get when you speak my name. She is the butterflies I felt inside when you asked me to speak of Love. Hers is the spice of Life that seasons the Bread I baked for you. She is the gentle kindness in the back massage that you gave me. It is by her hand that I painted my Toes your favorite colors or when I gave you my favorite Rose. She is the romantic thoughts that I think of you; the songs I sing of you when you are not with me in the Hills of France. Her hands write to you love letters from my heart; my lady lips quivering at the sound of your voice in my dreams. She shows my soul that I long to have you in me forever; even until our love runs thru the field and plays with her toys. Do not be afraid to know that you Love me my darling. Love loves those that truly Love her and she is in Love with those that are in Love with Her. For she is true in those that know her for what she is; she is the **purpose of Life in You**."*

It's with these thoughts that I reach beyond the word "Love" to a more fulfilling realization. A realization that Love is its own thing; that Love has its own purpose and power. I have come to believe that the word "LOVE" cannot ever be anything more than a mere shadow of the Living-Principle from which it is cast; because, by the Light of Truth such shadows always disappear.

I have heard it said of Christians that *"the Father so Loved the world; that he gave his only begotten Son"*. To this infinitely higher reference I give my reverence; to most others I am highly suspect. I do not presume to know the philosophy or belief of those who may read my short Essay. But, I do know this; there is a thought in our languages that points to a path of higher living, life ward toward greater *care and concern for each other, passion, commitment, gentleness, mutual trust & respect.*

To those who have said "That it is better to have loved and lost; than to never have loved at all"; I say that is your opinion. I am more inclined to suggest an earnest effort to understand the difference, and to pursue only the object of truth is all that matters. So to all those that find a more meaningful way to give expression to the true essence of the reference behind that wonderful word LOVE; I salute you.

_Jahbril

Undergrowth

While walking in a strange forest one day,
I observed the undergrowth in a rather thoughtful way.
> This is what I saw as I was
> Walking by and by...
A beautiful Eagle who would not try,
> Loaded with feathers and he would not fly!
"Your wings are as beautiful as the
> Mountain sky,
> Tell me my friend why won't you fly?"
Then I saw a Rose bud who neglected to grow, planted in
fertile ground and she would not grow! The ground was so
rich yet she would not show.

"O' tell me Rose, what do you say to the
> Rain and the Sun who feed you each day,
> Or the Wind and the Soil,
> Who sweated and fretted for you in great Toil?"

> Alas, I say dried bones by a pool,
> Covered in dust, the folly of fools.
> This was the Mind that refused to know,
> At an Oasis of Knowledge and yet would not
> Know.
> "Teach me O' Mind
> > That refuses to know,
> Show me sweet Rose
> > That refuses to grow,
> Tell me O' Eagle that refuses to fly,
> Where did it go, when did you die?"

-Jahbril

Grace Under Design

Grace is the splendor of a giant tree,
Gently swaying in the mountain breeze,
Deeply rooted and yet so free.
    Free to the eyes of you and me,
    To teach our hearts to hear and see.

"Meditate on my demonstration," said she, model my
natural mode.
    If you anchor your roots in the SOUL of your Soil,
    Spread your branches to the LIGHT;
    Then you shall see BEAUTY untold,
    The Grace of your DESIGN unfolds."

My Body's love is physical delight,
    But Mind is the Master Sense.
        My Soul craves Spiritual flight,
            ONE is the beautiful Present.
        Spirit is my Soul in flight,
    Mind is the Master Me.
Physique completes this divine design,
This I am and Be.

So, in the center of the depths of SOUL,
    In inner heights SPIRIT moves;

To give Living Love and Life,
    That hearts may be soothed.

Cease and release me O' ignorance,

Abandon me arrogant ways.
Flee from me vanity and vex,
Sin has end in evil days.

O' run to me and run with me,
Cry to me and fly with me;
Wisdom and Grace are life you see, Faith is the HOLY ONE.

-Jahbril

To Sow the Fallow Ground

To sow the fallow ground my friend, the fallow ground must be sown; to ride life's cycles around again, these truths must be known.

Open Minds on open Waves, receives the signs of those who save; beyond the Cross beyond the grave, is the fruit of the bold and the brave.

Throughout Time, in every Age, the seeds of Faith unfold in stages...

To sow the fallow ground my friend, the fallow ground must sown. To seek to live eternal again, hallow the fruits to be grown; For when the soil is rich and Sun light strong; when the the Rain is right and the Weeds are gone; Till the ground, O' hear the seed when Hate is bound the Soul is freed.

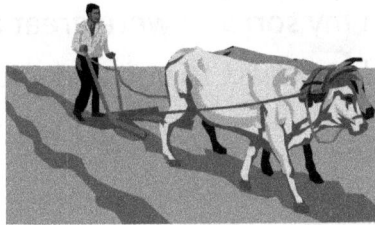

So, sow the fallow ground my friend and the fallow ground will be sown; Show the children love again and the Love will be shown in their Hope to fly, in their Heart to give, in their Courage to try, in their Will to live with Life Eternal.

In Praise of Living – LIFE

When I fell from my Mother's womb, I cried out to you and you caught me in tender Alms.

When my sorrows were great and strong, I turned my heart to you and you soothed me with beautiful Psalms.

Behold, when I knew my beloved's heart and understood it was you that I love, and then you blessed us.

When I first held your children near and gave thanks for they are so dear, behold my Soul called you Father.

When, I beheld your terrible Anger, on my face I fell where I stood, you lifted me in Love and understood my trembling.

Oh, how Beautiful are your Thoughts, how truly Wonderful is your Word. In Infinite depths and heights you wrought forever blessed are the Prayers whom you heard!

So ever incline my Heart to climb the scale, to your deepest Waters among the clouds. Incline you my Thoughts to clear the misty and mystic shroud.

For when my Mind began to know my Soul, My Soul revealed that Truth is ever just, and then I know that in all I ever do in you I AM to TRUST.

To Dance in the SERENGETI Rains

Columns of Life promenade on the Plains of the African stage; Colonnades of joy serenade the Rains to come again.

And with open arms the Sun calls the tides to the Dance of Life for the Earth, his Wife.

And the Light of the Ancient Thought said, "I saw the beautiful and brought the mist up to the sky. How I love to illuminate your World and elevate all the good things that you adore and ride the down pours all the way to Heaven's shore."

Then the Music came, a Serengeti Rain, the Cycle of Life without fear or strife. And the Dance was in Truth, so the Fruit took root once again.

The African SUN

As LIFE Lives...

So does the Sun give light and warmth. As LIFE lives, so does the Rain flow and falls to give all of the rainbow's end. As LIFE lives, so does the Soil fill the Earth with the fruits of a toil that the hand of Man can never spoil.

Who gave the Sun to the Trees; the Flower to the Bees; the Wave to Seas; the Soul to thee and me? Who gave the lion her claws; the Diamond it flaws; the Heart to the Mind; the Rhythm to Rhyme? Is there one provider to them all?

Whose handiwork does the Universe declare; who adorns this grace and power if you dare to know the Truth? There is an Infinite Power and Intelligence at the heart of the Whole. Who permeates and exceed all space and time; who gives habit and habitat to all according to clime. Who is the Father of all Forces and Master of all of Nature's Laws?

If you shall seek this Truth with your Whole Being, this very Truth will give you no rest until it fills your chest with Faith, anoint your Head with Wisdom, and direct your Hands and Feet to meet the purpose of your divine design. You shall be blessed to return to your aboriginal home whole and complete.

It is an astounding fact that LIFE itself makes provisions for ALL LIVING THING. "Consider the Ravens: for they neither sow nor reap; which neither have storehouse nor barn; and God feeds them; how much are you better than the fowls?" Luke 12:24

Now I ask you, "What common efforts and experiences do you share with all living things?" It is the effort to survive and progress that most common to all living things. That is every living organism must eat, drink, rest, reproduce, shelter and protect itself. And careful observation of Nature provides many clues to help point the way to Life's "Secrets of Success."

The Ancient Hebrew, King Solomon suggested, "Go to the Ant, you sluggard; consider her ways, and be Wise: which having no guide, overseer, or ruler, provides her meat in the summer, and gathers her food in the harvest. How long will you sleep, O sluggard? When will you arise out of your sleep?"

I recall one beautiful summer day not long ago, while on a nature walk, I observed for many hours several living creatures going about the serious business of survival. I noticed, for instance that the red-tailed hawks used a combination of natural tools, talents and techniques for hunting.

They often hunt from the air in forward moving spirals, patiently gliding for hours scoping out creeks and fields. In other instances, they chill out high in trees or on telephone lines to wait for food. And, when the opportunity comes they use their talons, sharp beaks and dives to progress.

Did you know that hawks and all other birds of prey must be taught how to use their wings, claws and beaks to survive? Did you know that those graceful swimmers the California Sea lions, which you see in zoos and aquariums, must be taught how to swim? In fact, if you take a sea lion pup and throw it in the water to soon it will surely drown.

Now if we humbly accept such clues from Nature and Scripture, it becomes clear that as sure as the Sun rises "LIFE itself makes provisions for ALL LIVING THINGS." And the whole business of living creatures or creations is to discover and use these provisions. This is the whole purpose in the principle of Learning; it is the application of the Law of Personal Growth.

Growth is the first Law of Life and emanates from the inside out. It is the unfolding of the Giant Redwood tree from the Cone; it is the releasing of the Eagle from the egg to the full fledges of flight. It is the liberation of the Man from the Child and the Angel from the Man; it is the opening out of the Woman from the girl to unfurl the peal in Nature's designs.

This expansion from a center along natural lines is the principle of the Progress operating in all living systems. In essence Growth is the unfolding of the possibilities latent in a thing. An entire forest of Oak trees lie awaiting the Acorn to take root in fertile soil and to absorb water and sunlight.

Notice that the Acorn does not have to create water, sunlight or soil; its responsibility is to take root and absorb these essential elements to stimulate those causes that preexist in it. And thereby, generating that natural order of progression that is necessarily its birth right. In brief, growth and development is the manifestation of potential along particular lines or specific purposes.

Now I am aware as I am writing these lines that you may not be familiar with the Natural Laws operating throughout All of Life and Nature, including you Life and Nature. Therefore, you may refer to my book, "The Keys to Solomon's Wealth" for more detailed treatment of this subject. It is very important that you acquire at least a lay persons understanding of the Natural Laws under which you live every moment of your life!

Growth is the first of these Laws. Therefore, let's outline some essential elements of this particular principle. First, I wish to impress upon your Mind, with all the sincerity and enthusiasm at my command, the tremendous importance of Growth to your Survival and Progress. By virtue of yet another Law of Life, anything and everything that does not grow will stagnate, decline and perish.

You will uncover this phenomena if you look, search; however, the current point is that you must expand, adapt, develop, release, apply, unfold, unroll and uphold yourself. You are a "Diamond in the Rough" which you must mine and refine into the Crown Jewel that your Mind really is!

So let's penetrate the Law of Growth a little more. Now in thinking of Growth I wish to encompass your whole nature; that is your mind, body and spirit or life. Physically most of your previous growth has been by a universal or generic principle which permeates all living creatures. You passed through certain natural stages of childhood, adolescence, etc. until you reached your present stature or features.

Mentally and spiritually you also grew by the same generic action of the principle; but manifesting itself in the form of a balance between social and genetic heredity. That is, you developed your beliefs, intellect, values, personality and character largely as a result of early contact with family and friends, teachers and preachers, television and radio or any other source of contact.

Now for many people this has been a very passive and receptive affair. They just kind of "Go with the Flow" and as the cliché goes, "The apple does not fall too far from the tree." Think for a moment about your own habits and beliefs, likes and dislikes; where did you originally get them?

Are they essentially your Father's or your Mother's? What, if any, church do you belong to and why? What political party do you support and why? What is your attitude about racial and cultural diversity? Why is your attitude what it is; media, parents or the sneers of peers?

Here is the point where you may begin to distinguish yourself from the great masses of Life's Creations. Notice that at the generic or universal level of manifestation, Life itself is careless of the individual and very careful of the species. It is manifested in the Laws of Nature as Natural Selection and Survival of the Fittest.

To assure the continuation of your kind kill or be killed; eat or be eaten is the predominate survival strategy in the generic process of nature. It is the principle of competition in its rawest form. Go to any major US Interstate and observe the war between the vines and the pines. They attack each other without hesitation or regret.

Think about this sobering, point for a moment and that which is arcane in your Soul shall recall its savage nature. You shall begin to understand more deeply the basis of humankind's ceaseless worship of violence and crime of every kind; our apparent bondage to the base end of the scale of nature.

Now if you will realize that Self-Preservation is the first Law of Nature and Growth is the first Law of Life, you will recognize the full import of self-development and personal growth. In other words, you will comprehend the full value of Self-Mastery.

You see it is a great maxim that life itself has made provisions for your survival and progress. But you must do the living and apprehend your talents, faculties and forces as your own with ever expanding proficiency. And, thereby more ably raise yourself then others above the principle of Competition toward the principle of Cooperation and Harmony.

You may not yet be accustomed to the idea that you are a whole consisting of unified parts. Think. The most distinguishing characteristic of LIFE is that it is living; therefore logic would suggest that by the principle of correspondence anything living at all must be in its essential nature a Life.

Given that you are living, you must be LIFE or that which lives. I know that the term "LIFE" is often used in the context of a set of experiences over time; but this is not what we would contemplate at this moment.

Think. What is your essential nature? What are you; yes you, who is reading these lines? Who are you? In whose "Image and Likeness" are you? Are you your clothes; Are you perhaps your body? Is that which I can detect of you with my five common senses all there is of you?

May I offer you a hint? You are so much more than any of the above mention things. I humbly offer you this suggestion; I sincerely hope you are able to accept it in the Spirit in which I offer it.

You are a LIFE! And as a Life, in the image and likeness of LIFE in itself, you are a Creator in your own space and time. You are the Operator of all your natural Forces and Powers. Try this brief experiment. Pick out any object that you can see right now and concentrate on it for approximately three minutes. Then close your eyes and recall the image of the object in your Mind's eye or Inner Vision. See it clearly. Then enlarge the image in your Mind to study its details. Turn it around and see the top, bottom and sides.

Now ask yourself, who is doing the watching? Who is doing the thinking and with what faculties? Who is operating your Inner vision? This is a very small example of your real position relative to your natural possessions. That is, you were provided with some natural forces and powers, whose sole intent or design is your survival and progress.

Furthermore, you could not alter or escape this truth one iota, whether through ignorance or design. This is your Divine Design and according to the nature of your knowledge and exercise of its features you create your predominate experiences.

Many souls and minds have gone through great trials and tribulations to get you to recognize and correctly apply this great truth. Many volumes of scared writings carry this point as their central purpose.

Many volumes of all manner sciences; including physical, mental and spiritual science carry this point as one of their underlying purposes. Thus throughout our study of history we encounter the ancient Axioms "Man, know thyself" and "If any Man glories, let him glory in this: That he knows and understands me [The Living-Life}."

I cannot think of a better reason to become familiar with the Living-Life, the All-Originating Life or Life in itself. To observe and experience this livingness in Life itself is one of Life's greatest pleasures. It is to begin to voluntarily co-operate and participate in the evolution of your own creation.

Therefore our position is that if we are to keep our "Eyes on the Prize" we should recognize that "Self-Mastery is the principle Prize." To give purpose to our thought and direction to our deeds. So, that we may rise like Living Waters to the level of our Source and enjoin the triumphs and trials of life with Hope and Faith. To this end my friend take all these clues and cues and endeavor to live your life as Life lives.

Affirmations in the Law of Personal Growth

1.   Specific Desire and Purpose>
I identify and prelive my specific major desire, purpose and goals in my imagination or mind's eye.

2.   Disciplined Imagination>
I recognize the Divine Power of imagination and put it to constructive use. I practice holding vivid images of goals and goal consequences on my "Mental Screen."

3.   Continuous Improvement>
I expand my Circle of Knowledge and Power through continuous learning and action. "Power of Knowledge in motion; Knowledge is Power at rest."

4.   Constructive Mental Attitude>
I open my Mind to positive, constructive stimuli and close it tight against negative, destructive stimuli. i.e. negative people, music, television or movies.

5.   Controlled Attention-Awareness>
I direct my attention towards thing relevant and important to my Life's Goals, Purpose and Direction.

6.   Self-Control>
I find positive, creative expressions of my emotions. I laugh or sing or dance or do anything that uplifts my mental states. I direct the power of my emotions to positive, constructive ends.

7. Sincerity and Enthusiasm>
I hold a genuine enthusiasm for the highest good of all living things. My thought and actions indicate my true, interior motive.

8. Self-determination>
I determine my own interest and thereby direct the power of my attention-awareness. "I am the active ingredient in personal experience."

9. Rest and Relaxation>
I restore my body's energy by maintaining a healthy balance between sleep and conscious physical activity.

10. Health and Fitness>
I pursue optimum health and fitness through regular, vigorous exercise.

11. Proper Diet and Nutrition>
I eat fresh fruits, vegetables, lean meats and dairy products in the quantities necessary to maintain optimum health for my age and height.

12. Family>
I give generously of my time and energy to help my family succeed and progress in a spirit love, harmony, cooperation and mutual understanding.

13. Community Service>
I give prudently of my time and energies to help make my community a better place to live and work.

14. Networking>
I seek and promote positive, constructive people and activities in the spirit of harmony and cooperation.

Unity>
I recognize the ecology and interdependence of all things
to one another; therefore I Think and Act toward others
the way that I would like them to Think and Act toward me.

15. Financial Control>
I build marketable proficiency and skills as the basis of my
livelihood. I strive to add value to my employer, customers
or clients through excellence, personal quality and service.

16. Meditation and Prayer>
I regularly engage in deep personal reflection, prayer and
meditation which sustain the development of my Sense of
Higher SELF and Purpose. I recognize the GOD given power
of thought and direct it to constructive use.

The Ethos of the Equinox

Balance. Rhythm. Equilibrium. Polarity. Wind and Wave; Body and Soul; Cradle and Grave; Young and Old. To center oneself with skill and understanding is one of LIFE's greatest clues to the secret of living. To rise higher and higher in the scale and to expand from a center is the objective of the Law of Growth. How many oaks are hidden in the acorn; how many sons are in the seed?

Nature favors those of dynamic focus, and clear direction. Natural adaptation; self-preservation; form following function, these reveal how the Creator imposes variety and splendor on the Creature. Yet, a unifying principle anchors the means to the ends. Birds and bees, songs and seas, flowers and trees all add their particular color to the rainbow and bring balance to the spectrum.

Symmetry is the song that gives harmony to opposites; such as left and right, man and woman, thought and act. While reflecting on these truths, the Mind begins to recognize the unifying principle operating within itself. Conscious to subconscious, right brain to left, the awakening is at first very imperceptible. When the vision in the valley comes home the unity has begun to complete itself.

Woes to those stumbling through life with one mind tied behind their back. Such ignorance and arrogance is a deep ill that would break the Law and extinguish the Light. How many Souls will it take to unfold you? Hermes Trismegistus, Imhotep, Moses, Solomon, Jesus, Mohammed, Ghandi, Emerson, Howard Thurman, Martin L. King or many thousands else?

In the gap between your thoughts giants dwell in the unified field. Peace and power, serenity and harmony open the gate wide to all who would enter. What can be plainer? What else needs to be spoken to you?

Your meditation is concentration of a peculiar type. But, be not overly chained to this religion or that philosophy; be not overly bound to this school or that science. But, merely open your own mind and knock on the door with firm determination.

Sincerity and faith will receive you with psalms of joy and tears of laughter. The Universe is an open book for open minds closed to evil and unwarranted fears. Behold life living. Purpose is fused in every design. How are you made; are you a Mind?

Mon'Ami, I deeply pray that you see and hear the song the Angels sing for you. For every time you see the sign the Light shines through to balance you in the True.

For this is
the Ethos of the Equinox.

The Nature of Friendship

I have long desired to write an essay on Friendship; because from my very earliest years it seems to stand out among the many forms of virtue and riches. In writing of friendship, I am referring to the interior relation between heart and mind, where each seeks the highest good of the other. Sincerity, genuiness, mutual-respect, acceptance, kindness and mutual-understanding all merely clothe the real, interior nature of this giant emotion.

Real friendship is unity in its dual form. It is heart and mind; wisdom and faith; spirit and soul; sun and moon; heaven and earth it is the I in I. It is as the oil that anoints the head; it is a natural emollient soothing the pains and burden of Truth. It can never be faked and those who would seek to do so invariably destroy their own souls. For the soul seeks truth, life, love and light; so the soul seeks escape from lies, death, hate and ignorance.

There appears to be a certain kinship in friendship. It is a peculiar feeling of brotherly or sisterly love; yet it is often found dwelling deep within the hearts and minds of many who are of no official relations. I find this an intriguing paradox. Who befriends the battered wife, the abused daughter, the confused son or the misused husband? What manner of friendship is open them all?

It is this: When you mind has your heart in mind, and your heart has your mind in heart you are standing in the threshold. When you seek the good in everyone you meet, you are becoming unfolded. When you earnestly and sincerely seek to befriend the trees, the birds and the bees, the sun and the seas, you are walking into the light. When your heart's mind is in deep desire of your Creator you are living in love aright.

There are not many who can say with truth and understanding that they are in a friendship; for to do so is to recognize the Unity in all living things. Because many minds are afraid of truth, they are asleep in a deep fear. I have seen those in whom the seeds of a unique brand of friendship attempts to sprout. They actually shuttered with fear and doubts, foolish denial and unenviable shouts of quiet desperation.

It is a great truth that real friendship radiates from the inside, like brilliant sun light on a beautiful autumn afternoon; it is a profound feeling of self-fulfillment and self-completion. This intrinsic condition is the surest possible foundation of all meaningful relationships. It is like the small voice of the giant called Intuition that seeks to correct many a wayfarer.

Therefore my friend, it appears imperative to me to cultivate, and stimulate this brand of thinking. How you may ask does one go about such an endeavor? Seek to know intimately the purpose of life, love and light. A living soul from days of old explained it in these words, "Seek you first the Kingdom of God and all these things shall be added unto you." And also, "the Kingdom of Heaven is within you."

Self-Encounters of the First Kind

Brother will you spare a dime; I need your Love to buy some wine. But, spare me pity and hold your speech; I need your Light that I may reach yonder corner liquor store to endure my pain a little more.

Now if you will help me repair my breech and do no wrong here, don't you preach... I need your Life that I may live to be a friend, the one to give you...

My brother, as I stand in deed in your stead, I do concede when I met you on the corner street it was not easy to not reach.

Now my Mind our lines instruct:

Let Character and Conduct state my Faith and lift thee up;

Let Sincerity and Pure intent find my deeds the perfect vent;

And let the Power to explain seek my Heart to Proclaim: Of all I say and all I know it matters most what I show.

Choice and Consequences

There are many love stories in the annals of world literature; but precious few of them lift our hearts to the level of love embracing choice and consequences, cause and effects. I say that Romeo and Juliet are the enmity as compared. Ramses II and Nefertiti were as bitter enemies held against the light of this truth. Don Juan cold never be as charming to the maidens as choice is to its consequences.

I am often intrigued by this deep commitment. It is a relationship that refuses the possibility of divorce. No strong wind, no hard tears, no other lover can long break the grip of this powerful affinity.

Nature's law of attraction, cause and effect, and retaliation in kind all testify of a strong bond of love. Consequences seek choice like flowing water seeks the level of its source. Watch the infatuation of the sun to the trees or the rose to the bees and you shall understand.

When I was younger, I recall the impression of the story of Genesis in my Bible: Choice is among the first in order of the natural forces and faculties present in humankind. It sets all the other powers to work in the direction of its force. It mattered little to me whether the Book of Genesis was allegory or history; the primary import is the enormous of consequence to its choice.

There are those among minds, who fancy that they shall break this bond and disassociate these truest of lovers. However, just as water temporarily parted by the wave of a hand will soon return to perfect its unity; so **does** choice reunify and completes itself.

The experiences encountered in life frequently express one's degree of self-mastery in the direction of our decisions or choices. For instance, to choose a positive, constructive attitude is to choose all the predominating consequences of the choice. Furthermore, to decide to think and act healthy is to be healthy. So it is to remember and always take heed as often as we are able to the consequences of our choices. Cause and effects are united in deep love; as choice and consequences are bound together passionate embrace. May we keep this forever in our hearts as we choose our parts in life?

Freedom in Chains

I see Freedom in chains behind the Eyes of a dove; A Love
encaged at the moment of Love.

Wings clipped and bound, a Song without sound; a fright
with the right of a beautiful flight.

I see Grace under the pressure of a lessor urge that drains
and enchains the Tide's inward surge. . .

A Heart on the verge of Spiritual truth; A Soul in the fold of
a Tree with deep roots.

I see Serenity and Peace at the feet of the Vain; Virtue is
washed away by the trouble in the rain.

And Lo' there is Elegance and Taste in the arms of Waste to
hasten the Life to the bonds of strife.

Alas, there are the Children of Love in the Iron Glove of
Hate; a fate they relate to their parental estate. . .

What more can I say; but turn to the Way and the Night of
Day and the Power in Peace. To set Freedom free, lift up
the Grace, embrace Elegance with Taste and come to know
there's space in the Truth for the Free to Free.

Signals

Power lines, from rhyme to Mind, Carrier Waves on a sea sublime. Vibrations sent and received; Modulation caught and perceived.

Signals? You better believe it.

Thoughts resonate time after time, permanent waves from Mind to Mind, bringing Truth or foolish lines.

Long distance? It doesn't matter; for instance, Doug Chatter MC is a mix'n; so the beat is the heat and you're fix'n to tap your feet. Now the rhythm and rhyme has got your Mind; permanent wave'n got you misbehave'n long after the line is far behind.

Whose thoughts are those? "I can't; so I don't", Could you tell me please? "I could; but I won't."

Stick ups and Interconnections, Look up and do some personal reflection.

Radio Waves and Television you see, can make you a slave or bring you Mastery; which do you want to be?

-Soh Phari

A Troubling Rain

A troubling rain played the window pain, as I sat alone in the crowd at the west end of the bar; behold, though it was Noon in the sky was the Moon, and the Sun was somewhere afar.

When suddenly my Mind was inclined to a dream of this kind.

In the back of a bitter room, in the dark of the Noon she stared out the window with Hope none too soon.

But, in quiet desperation, she coldly waved the Sun good-buy again.

Then as the east Wind came to stir up the flames, so came I to stimulate her thought; for behold I saw her mingling laughter with the fears that she brought.

"Life and Light!" said I with a radiant smile; when suddenly it came, the Sun for the Rain. O how beautiful is that which was wrought! Then Tears of Fear turned to smiles of cheer.

When I refocused my Thought to see what troubled the rain, behold I stood in the Noon sky once again.

The Prodigal Sun

Umoja

The Thought is in the Ether; O' the WORD is on this page, open your Heart's Mind to the Soul of the Sage.

In every Age, in every Time, there is a sign with Truth sublime to unfold talent latent Minds.

Vibration, in the ethereal night, desperation, in mystical flight, ungrounded fear and frustration is darkness to the Light.

I and I, Thoughts are Things. Bye and bye, the Truth shall ring. Living Hope is the Soul that sings from days of old: "Know Thyself."

If I am a Thought, how am I employed? If I am a Truth, why am I ignored? If I am a Life, where is my embrace; When shall I and I dance, face to face?

In the morning, when I rise shall my Soul be surprised to make wise and clear the Heart?

SUN rise

In Tears of Prayer

All praise and glory to you, O great and awesome one; Honor and power are thine. Hold my hand Lord unless I drown in the tears of my sorrow; my errors overflow me. My Soul is bent. My heart is broken and bare. How can I live without you? For even the grass of the field must have sunshine, even the lily must have rain; every root makes this plain. Even so are you to me; where can I go without you, what can I be?

O Lord, righteousness belongs unto thee; but unto me, confusion of face as at this day. O Lord, to me belongs confusion of face; I am all together wounded because of my sins and the sins of my fathers. Fools wear my crown, jackals dance upon my Diadem, whores run my dreams aground, my light is fading and dim. They laugh and love to scorn me; I am in bitter sorrows.

Why have I hated your knowledge? How could I have slain you Prophets and precepts? In who have I placed my trust; dust is my bed Father. I did not heed your call and forgot your laws of the days of my youth when Mind had not reclined in lust.

You alone are wonderful and good; you who is the ALL and ONE. You have done all your vows, your promise is in your hand, none can make it void. You created a great garden, in a world of sparkling waters and placed my Spirit in the midst of love, beauty, joy and peace. You built my fortress and created me as a strong lion. Giant suns are as a twinkling of an eye to you and Aeons are like fleeting moments; yet you can call my atoms by name.

O Lord save me, unless I put my Trust in my understanding. Be you my God of my strength. Write your law into my heart and engrave your purpose deep within my mind. I beseech you Father, do not give me over to my foolishness; but teach my thoughts to stay on you.

For I confess to you this day, I know of nothing more beautiful than Beauty itself; neither can I conceive of anyone wiser that Wisdom; nor do I perceive any love greater that Love; neither do I believe any light is more revealing than Light; not any depth more concealing than the Deep Darkness. Of all that you shall do through me and to me, if it be not impious to ask, grant me this one blessing: That I shall always love you with all my Heart, with all my Mind, with all my Soul and all my Strength.
AMEN

Magnets and Mastery

In a land of Visions and Rhythms, far beneath the Night, where sleep liberates daydreams from afternoon daylight and songs carry on new rhythms, of Magnetic delight

I heard it said if lyrics are read at this moment of Spiritual Insight, a new day is sure to dawn in the morning's twilight.

But then I heard one yell, "Awake me now, for this land can be Heaven or it can be Hell!"

Then a familiar voice cried out, Mastery is your Birthright; but you must choose well.

For then we can become fully awake and finally cease to wait for I AM...Master in your Kingdom of Influence, Prudent in your matters of Prudence, Wise to meet

your needs, Faithful to complete the
Holy deeds of your design for I AM...

Thoughts are Tools

The Creative Nature of Thought is a monumental subject which I can only hope to scratch the surface in this brief discourse. However, a little observation and research will reveal to you that humankind, of all living creatures under the sun, has been given many provisions to survive and progress. That is Life itself has invested humankind with natural tools suited to accomplishment of certain purposes. Thought is the first in order and importance of these tools.

What role does thought play in your life's experiences? Is your thought working for you or against you? Science and history has long established the preeminent role of thought in the course of human development. Everything that has ever been created by the human mind originated in thought. Every building, every song, every street, every wrong, everything ever created by humankind emanated from thought.

Thought may be broadly categorized in two classifications, namely conscious or voluntary and subconscious or involuntary. Each form is intricately designed to serve a particular range of purpose. That is, voluntary thought corresponds to the conscious phase of mind and involuntary thought, such as intuition or "hunches" correspond to the subconscious.

Most education institutions are designed to develop abilities to use your conscious thought powers to solve problems, make decisions and take action. However, they largely ignore the stupendous capability of your subconscious thought. To increase your ability to apply both phases of your mind is to gain the use of the greatest tool known to humankind, the awakened mind, your Diamond Mind!!!

Chapter one in the book "The Keys to Solomon's Wealth" by your present author, describes some methods by which you may tap the giant power of your subconscious mind, in addition to your conscious mind to generate ideas, solve-problems and make decisions. Imagination and thought, technology and "smart work" will transform your ideas into reality, problems into solutions and decisions into destiny.

Today's use of tools and techniques mark a significant milestone in the development of the human mind. Our technologies have enabled us to comprehend more, faster than ever before. Physical tools and technologies, which are created in thought, are extensions of your hands and feet, extending the effects of your labor. Therefore, you can plant and harvest food crops faster with mechanical tools, than you could by hand.

The transmutation of thoughts into technology and ideas built sprawling ancient cities and nations, such as Babylon, Thebes, Ur, Ramses and Pithom. Archaeological finds revealed detailed architecture in these cities. Egypt's great pyramids uncover a masterful combination of the power of human ingenuity and the technology of that particular age. There continues to be much debate in our present age about how such magnificence and precision could have been achieved so long ago.

However, every major age in the recorded history of man, uncovered the advantages of possessing technologically advanced tools of that age. For instance, the use of fire made early humans far more powerful those other animals. Suddenly man could remove unwanted vegetation, cook food, warm shelters and better protect him.

The same observation has been true in the conduct of wars between nations. That is, whichever armies have blended technological advantage with advance mental tactics have won most often.

Enormous quantities of evidence to support this fact have been uncovered in many caves, tombs and monuments of antiquity. Egyptian hieroglyphics display engineers and laborers employing advanced techniques in art, war and construction. All initiated in thought.

"First the Thought, then the Thing."

Before Imhotep, an ancient Egyptian multi-genius, had laid one brick on the famous Step pyramid, he developed an idea or a blueprint of the final structure in his mind. He then transformed this blueprint into building instructions. Whereon, he combined these initial representations of his thought with the best tools and technologies available in his age, and by that transmuting his idea into physical reality.

Before Garrett A. Morgan developed the first traffic light, he had a clear idea of it in his mind. He transformed this idea into blueprints and instructions, by then allowing the invention to be manufactured into physical reality. You see so many traffic lights today that it's very easy to forget their value.

Charles Drew first conceived of the idea and the method to store human blood in "blood banks" in his mind. By that, saving countless lives over many years of war and disease. He transformed his thought from an idea into a physical reality.

Today you can observe hundreds of inventions or ideas that have been transformed into reality. Watch such programs as "Beyond 200" and "Invention" for many more examples. What do your television set, telephone, job and your house have in common? All these items began in someone's mind as a thought!

Many high achievers have reported over the ages that the technique they used to employ their thought is visualization. Visualization or voluntary imagination is a potent way to use the creative powers of your thought to help you achieve goals. Disciplined imagination will amplify your efforts and magnify your personal and professional development.

Take some time to develop a detailed scene of your specific goals and desire in the state of accomplishment; that is imagine that you have already done them. Make certain that you include sensory stimuli, such as the aroma of colognes or perfumes, the taste of foods, the sound of people congratulating you, and the sight of the scene. The more vivid, sensory detail you include the clearer the picture is to your mind of the condition that you are giving it to create.

Visualization works best when it is done over a period of time when you are very relaxed, preferably before bed, and your vision is emotionally compelling for you. Do not be afraid to really get into your vision; make it a habit. You will be very surprised at the results!

Are you using it in cooperation and harmony with the source and origin of this greatest of boons? Do you desire to expand your mastery and influence over your conditions? Then my friends I say to you take liberally of the provisions given you, with every expanding skill and understanding and "Live as Life lives."

I Sojourn I

On the Inner Road I hold that Love glows above the Sun and runs like Living Waters.

On the Inward Journey, Light overflows many Rainbows without end.

On the Interior Quest, the bold and blessed Travelers reach for the Highest Self to rest in the Wealth of Life.

Inside of Life, you will find Love Giving;
Inside of Love, you will see Life Living;

Inside of Light, you will be surprised how the Road opens wide to the All.

"I live every day, one day at a time, by the miracle of the present moment; deeply rooted in my past, firmly moving to my future. I live the miracle of Life."

-Jahbril

Imani

And the child said, "Speak to me of faith and failures."

"Imani", replied Hope "you shall not always fear your failures; but shall grow to love them. Count it all joy when you shall fall into various trials; knowing this, that the testing of your faith works patience. But let patience have her perfect work, that you may be perfect and entire, lacking nothing.

If any mind lack wisdom, let it ask of God, who gives to all liberally and upbraids not, and it shall be given. But let that mind ask in faith, nothing wavering. For one that wavers is like a wave of the sea driven with the wind and tossed. For let not that mind thinks that it shall receive anything of the Lord.

A double-mind is unstable in all of its ways. Let the brother of low degree rejoice in that he is exalted; but the rich, in that he is made low, because as the flower of the grass he shall pass away. For the sun is no sooner risen with a burning heat, but it withers the grass, and its flowers fall and the grace of the fashion of it perishes; so also shall the rich mind fade away in his ways.

Blessed is the mind that endures failure; for when it is tried, it shall receive the crown of life, which the Lord has promised to them that love him. Hold these truths always in your thoughts; do not let is escape. Blessed is the mind that keeps its thoughts stayed on faith to benefit from failure."

As SPIRIT Leads

On the open void, in the Quantum Field, Spirit bade the Soul to yield.

With tender Psalms, and out stretched Arms Spirit made the Soul to live.

Spirit, on Living Waters, placed the SUN and Moon in order upon the waves without border.

As Spirit leads, One goes, natural Thoughts in Mystic flows.

So in the center of the depths of Soul, Spirit moves Earth and Sky; to reveal Natural Modes to the hearts of I and I.

Psalms 40

1 I waited patiently for the Lord; he inclined to me and heard my cry. **2** He drew me up from the desolate pit, out of the miry bog, and set my feet upon a rock, making my steps secure. **3** He put a new song in my mouth, a song of praise to our God. Many will see and fear, and put their trust in the Lord. **4** Happy are those who make the Lord their trust, who do not turn to the proud, to those who go astray after false gods. **5** You have multiplied, O Lord my God, your wondrous deeds and your thoughts toward us; none can compare with you. Were I to proclaim and tell of them, they would be more than can be counted. **6** Sacrifice and offering you do not desire, but you have given me an open ear. Burnt offering and sin offering you have not required. **7** Then I said, "Here I am; in the scroll of the book it is written of me. **8** I delight to do your will, O my God; your law is within my heart." **9** I have told the glad news of deliverance in the great congregation; see, I have not restrained my lips, as you know, O Lord. **10** I have not hidden your saving help within my heart, I have spoken of your faithfulness and your salvation; I have not concealed your steadfast love and your faithfulness from the great congregation. **11** Do not, O Lord, withhold your mercy from me; let your steadfast love and your faithfulness keep me safe forever. **12** For evils have encompassed me without number; my iniquities have overtaken me, until I cannot see; they are more than the hairs of my head, and my heart fails me. **13** Be pleased, O Lord, to deliver me; O Lord, make haste to help me. **14** Let all those be put to shame and confusion who seek to snatch away my life; let those be turned back and brought to dishonor who desire my hurt. **15** Let those be appalled because of their shame who say to me, "Aha, Aha!" **16** But may all who seek you rejoice and be glad in you; may those who love your salvation say continually, "Great is the Lord!" **17** As for me, I am poor and needy, but the Lord takes thought for me. You are my help and my deliverer; do not delay, O my God.

A Gift of the Wind

It seems that time after time, the Wind brings that unique line of Thought on a special day, which lights the Path and shows you the Way.

Yes, with gems in hand and pearls so grand how priceless is that which is brought?

It is finer than Gold and ever so bold; It is the principle thing that is taught.

It is the Diamond of Life, the
Emerald of Love, the Sapphire of
Light, and the Truth from Above.

It is far finer than Wine, it is the
fruit in the line. "There is no other
time like the beautiful and ever
PRESENT..."

At the Top of the Truth

Once in a while when the day goes away, I feel my Heart aching to say...

When the Moon is blue and my eyes are red my Soul is left empty from the vision which said...

When my Silence is sweet, Quietness is strong and Peace is a release from the long journey to the highest Virtues...

I say meet me at the Top of Truth; see me at the foot of His Throne.

Far above the ego trips, deep below the surface drips hear me say I was "Wrong".

\-

Forgiven

UJAMAA

And the children said, "Speak to us of cooperation."

"Ujamma", replied Hope "you must let harmony and mutual support abound among you. Do not seek your interest selfishly; but desire to benefit each other. Hold your heart away from jealously and do not let contention spoil your profit.

And be not forgetful to be pleasant to strangers; for thereby some have entertained angels unawares. Remember those that are bonds, as if you are bound with them; those who suffer adversity, as being yourselves also in their body.

Be whole within yourselves and know your own thoughts. Whatever things are true, whatever thing are honest, whatever things are just, whatever things are pure, whatever things are lovely, whatever things are of good report; if there be any virtue or praise in it, think on these things. For a mind is what it thinks all the day long.

Finally, think of each other as you would have it thought of you. Be of one mind, even as the ALL is one mind. For herein sleeps the secret to all of your Power and Virtue.

TIME

To everything there is a season, and a time to every purpose under the heaven:

Make time to listen; it is the source of Knowledge.

Make time to Think, it is the true College.

Make time to Play, it is the key to good Health.

Make time to Work, it is the price of Wealth.

Make time to give, it is a rare Pearl.

Make time to Pray, it is the strength in the World.

Make time to Laugh, it is music to the Soul.

Make time to Cry, it is the secret of the bold.

To everything there is a season, and a time to every purpose under the heaven.

To the Inner Woman

Lovely and pure my flower, is the fragrance of your thoughts; Wonderful and secure are they when to my Heart's Mind they are brought.

Bold and Beautiful I say are you when in silent sleep; for your Heart is so full of gold, your dreams must be honey sweet.

I do adore and desire you; my hope is to inspire you and love you ever more.

Who are you, O' who are you and what are you sent to do?

Are you come on the wings of Wisdom to calm the storms of Time? Are you come of some great accord to stimulate my wearied Mind? Perhaps you were hidden in my ribs, to show me later great truths sublime?

In the "Songs of Spring" my Soul did sing until the heights of summer; so again I pray that I hear you say "I've come to share with you my highest honor."

-Jahbril

Songs of Spring

How lovely is your voice my dove, how beautiful are your songs. May I have your hand in marriage, for I must not wait too long?

O' give me of Wisdom to wife, and Understanding as my lover, Courage and Respect for Life, and Prudence as my brother.

For ignorance I can't endure. So add of Wisdom to my side and my life shall be insured.

Keep foolish pleasure and vain conceit, for vanity is to defeat foolish souls. Give my heart to Understanding, let me be her concubine. Give my Soul to Diligence and Faith, as my favorite Valentines.

Let Instruction be our wedding gift, Peace and Joy to lift my burdened Soul. For then shall I endure this world's suffering and toil.

I thank you LORD for the Light of your
anointed, ONE gave for us his life.

You lead them all by Wisdom and Faith, to
save us all from our
corruption through Grace.

The Eros of Moonlight

O' the Moonlit waters
Are serene and calm,
By the hand of the Sun,
Left peaceful and warm.
As Mind comes to
Heart
and Spirit to the Soul,
so comes Wind to the Waves,
sweeping and bold.
A primordial dance,
an ancient romance
in splendor and grace,
to embrace the light
and hold the sight long
O' the
moment is right
when the
Moon lit the
night at the kiss of the
Sun;
to go inside the Light
and swim as One.
For Life opens the Right
so that Truth can run,
and set Freedom free
to perfect Liberty;
and liberate the Mind
to elevate the Heart
and orchestrate the Chimes,
to resonate the Harp
and enshrine the Soul,
of I and I.

Wisdom of Faith

O Wisdom, if you would be water, I shall dive deeply in you, to find the hidden keys to your devotion.

> Wisdom of the ages, if you should be strong drink, I shall soon drown in your intoxication.

Love do not fail me, Desire do not leave me, O soul she is your life she is your life O soul, she is your life.

> O Faith in God, if you will be my snare, I shall run to you, that I might not escape; for your prison is his Kingdom.

Faith in the Ancient of Days, if you will be my blood, I shall cherish you as the life of my life, that you may flow forever as the spirit of my veins, the hope of my freedom.

> Passion do not fail me, for I need her. Hope do not leave me; I plead for her. O soul she is your life, she is your life O soul, she is your life.

You Wisdom of Faith, you Faith of Wisdom are the beauty most; yet like a ghost you cannot be seen by those that will not see.

> O daughter of Wisdom, you daughter of Faith, your beauty should shine in my Soul and my Mind, your love to wife is the hope of my life.

Your bosom and thighs are the desire of my eyes that I may be yours forever, in my Heart's Mind.

Diligence

Diligence and Determination, Perseverance and Persistence these are the hallmarks of greatness. Those who would dare to break the true bonds of Freedom to wear the Crown of Self-Mastery must give purpose to their Thought and direction to their Deeds. A personal pledge to one's highest self, to unfold latent talents, will awaken mighty forces sleeping deep within oneself to bring success. Focused Action and Persistency of Purpose is beautiful music to Minds opened long ago. And if your Heart is dedicated to your highest ideals toward all other living things, Life itself is moved to bring your Heart in tune with Infinity. Many lives have lived this truth, and many more shall live it; so of all the good that you would do, set your

Heart to see it through.

The Principal Prize

For many centuries, archeologists, historians, conquerors, tourist and thieves searched the lands of ancient Egypt in search of treasures particular to their interest. They scoured the Nile Valley in pursuit of Riches, Power and Knowledge. The Royal Valley, where the Pharaohs were buried, was particularly hard hit. Much of the booty has found its way to the British Museum and other private and public institutions.

There are those who argue that perhaps it were best that these places had been left undisturbed. Nevertheless, as fortune or misfortune would it, we have a glimpse into the lives and character of some of the world's highest achievers.

What Character and Characteristics caused Egypt to flourish for over four-thousand years? I was amazed when I first became aware of the material wealth of such Pharaohs as Ramesses II, Thutmoses III or Tutankhamen. How could anyone have obtained such vast fortune and power? This question held my attention for at least a couple of years.

Eventually, I realized that the answers to my questions were carved in almost every stone in Egypt and supported by every major holy writing in the world. That is the answers were in the content, purpose and objectives of the hieroglyphs. It was as if my Mind said, "If you stop looking at the Fool's Gold you will see the True Gold!" They possessed other forms of wealth of power than material riches!

"Knowledge is Power at rest; Power is Knowledge is motion."

-Jahbril

Then I understood the meaning of Proverbs, Chapters 2 and 3. Power expressed in the form of continuous action, is the basis of personal growth and all enduring achievement.

Therefore I submit that Self-Mastery is the highest state of Personal Growth; it is the Principal Prize. That is, Self-Mastery is that state of personal growth and development that empowers one to live their potential.

According to Dr. Maulana Karenga, author of The HUSIA, ancient Kemetic *Geru* or Self-Masters, embodies this truth in an ideal character type which centered on Self-Control, Wisdom, Piety, and other important virtues that characterized *Maat*. Maat was the overall model of ideal conduct, morals and ethics in all aspects of Egyptian life.

Many other historians and archaeologist confirm that this state of personal development was essential to both the practical and spiritual aspects of Kemetic culture. It was the basis for obtainment of the loftiest goals. It represented the character type which corresponded to high achievement.

By the light of Self-Mastery, a fundamental principle of Maat, Imhotep designed the fabulous Step Pyramid of Pharaoh Djoser. Many of the remnants of the Kemetic Egypt bear witness to master Mathematicians, Healers, Architects, Agriculturists and Strategist. Names like Ramose II, Akhenaton, Tutankhamen, Thutmoses II, and

Hatshepsut seem to reverberate even until today from the grandest ancient monuments in the history of the world.

Any serious, open minded study of the attitudes, characteristics and habits of all of Africa's great achievers will find the principles of Self-mastery shining forth like a beacon in the dark. Therefore, modern scientists like Dr. Dennis Kimbro, Dr. Maulana Karenga and Dr. Ivan Van Sertima continue to advocate Self-Mastery or Self-Empowerment as the most desired state of personal development for the same reasons that the ancient Egyptians advocated it. It is the root and genesis of all enduring, human progress!!

Personal mastery of anything is a matter of degree of skill and experience. So do not be concerned if you have not mastered yoga or painting or dance or anything else. Continuous improvement effort is the means by which you will increase your level of expertise and build the habits necessary for mastery.

A characteristic of your reflex nerve system is that whenever you repeat a thought or act, especially in highly emotional states, it becomes more and more involuntary. In other words, anything that you repeat under any given condition will become a conditioned response, an automatic reflex. This is the mechanism and force by which you create the color and quality of your life's experiences.

What are the experiences of students with good study habits? What are the experiences of athletes with good practice habits? Are they winners or loser? You see, personal achievement may be defined as the result of life enriching habits.

Therefore, habit is a potent, interior force that living-life provided you to aid our survival and progress. Through habit force the subconscious mind controls all your vital systems; thereby allowing you conscious mind to focus on further progress. This is one of life's clues to successful living. Your subconscious mind is the seat of power for all your automatic functions; including the mental, physical, and spiritual operations of your being.

Now if you have recognized the suggestions that thought has an inherent tendency to transform itself into its physical reality, and this is true beyond any reasonable doubt, you recognize the power that the force of habit imposes on your life. This is a very important truth that you can never escape, whether through ignorance or design. Our habit force my friend, is indeed worthy of mastery. What are your habits?

In Touch with the Infinite

What is the greatest power available to humankind? Is it nuclear energy? Electricity? Is it magnetic propulsion? Or perhaps it is some undiscovered form of energy? For many centuries humanity has searched the earth and heavens for greater means of acquiring desired ends; exploring the depths of the oceans, heights of the air and even the immense frontiers of the human mind.

In this manner, humankind is uncovering and applying stupendous powers, forces and faculties. For instance, it has been noted that if the earth was twenty-four hours old, humankind would only have appeared in the last second. In this relatively short period, human progress has extended from the splendid Egyptian civilizations of ancient Africa to the exploits of modern science beyond Mars. Inventions like airplanes, electric light, space shuttles, psychology, astronomy; mathematics and art stud the path of human development.

However, of all the forces and faculties that have been uncovered so far, there is an ever widening realization of one all-embracing power which underlies, unifies, permeates and integrates all things. Imagine if you will, the time before anything in the manifested universe came into being; when darkness was upon the face o the deep. A perfect unity, laden with all possibility, dwelt in a state of undifferentiated potential. All intelligence, all powers, all forces, all bodies, all creatures everything in existence today originated from this ultimate reality.

Beyond doubt, this primary reality is the plenum for all that has ever been all that is and all that will ever be. It is boundless, inexhaustible, omniscient, and omnipotent. It manifests itself as a dazzling array of intricate, interconnected systems in the universe.

For instance, it creates countless millions of stars, some several times bigger than our sun, as the center of complete solar systems. And it sets these systems in motion according to a dizzying array of cosmic laws. Furthermore, it created a brain and nervous system capable of contemplating itself and its ultimate source. That is, it created the human system.

This power has been both denied and revered under many names and in as many ways. Yet the underlying truth remains supreme, pressing ever onward the thrust of its unlimited energy.

It is described as the primary, first cause that is both one and all things. It is one in that is whole and complete in itself. It is all in that all things are subsequent to it. It is primary, first cause in that it is antecedent to every other action. It is that infinite intelligence and power that is self-generated, all embracing LIFE. This is the greatest power available to humankind.

I have often wondered why we tend to reflect those things which we contemplate. Calm waters at night in quiet moments seem to soothe the soul, ease the heart and relax the mind. Peace, harmony, tranquility and serenity are divine songs of love to the weary. Thoughts of peace and power tend to render a mind peaceful and powerful.

Melodious music has power to bring one in tune with its mystical vibrations

I know of no other object or subject closer to the needs of the human heart than primary, living-life. Most sacred literature in the history human development, urge listeners to study and meditate on the divine life; thereby applying the principle that one grow to reflect that with one contemplates. By this mysterious power of thought the creature finds itself in tune with its Creator.

Genesis

"When your spirit moved upon the face of the water Genesis declared your omniscience; when I was conceived in darkness I slept in the womb of all understating. Then the Living-Life brought me to birth and revealed to me my potential. The Tree of Life was betrothed my Wife; yet when I chose the Tree of Knowledge for my College, the strength of my trust covered me in dust."

We shall not always esteem wisdom above faith; or trust over understanding; or explanation before experience. Rather we shall learn the truth in unity; the complement in opposites; the symmetry in polarity. You see the whole is the sum of the parts synergized to set the system alive with rhythm and balance.

The Universe is an open book to open minds; when you seek its beauty and virtue it shall seek you too. For behold a truth; The Universe shall once again recognize itself in you. Must you understand combustion before you drive a car? Must you know quantum physics before you enjoy a shuttle launch; or should you understand the nature of time before you own a watch?

Yet, faith to the faithful is the substance of hope; the evidence of things unseen. Faith. Trust and experience are natural correlative of wisdom, understanding, and knowledge. When we trust the trustworthy, we experience the truth in the laws of nature. Faith without evidence or substance; Trust without knowledge is a hazard and a danger at best.

History is replete with this lesson often forgotten and seldom learned: Adolph Hitler, Jim Jones, Bonito Mussolini and how many others will it take? Is the stage set when the number of his name shall attain the fame proclaimed of him? Which shall save you knowledge or faith; or shall it be the unified power of the whole truth, the way and the Life?

The ignorant can never be safe; but neither can the wise nor the strong; nor can the world be totally safe from any of these very long. A heart without prudence and the mind unbalanced by love is a sandy shore unfit to hold the foundation of your temple. Surely, a savage wind will soon rend your hopes in pieces with great joy at your folly.

Who can reach your truth or expose you to the roots of darkness in light? Who can love for you or live for; cry for you or give for you, however try they might? Look how you breathe, your interior-light is burning and living on unobtrusive. Peace, be still and quiet if you will; for in this you may feel that centering moment, when wisdom and faith blend into one silence.

When shall I again encompass all knowledge? When heart and mind in divine love entwine; when wisdom and faith in spirit and grace, shows me the way; when knowledge and trust do as they must and raise me from the dust to acknowledge my image and likeness. So shall it be for all don't you see; for the all is one in thee and me.

Adam

Diamind

Your Network Advantage

How many times have you heard the old cliché, "It's not what you know; but who you know? "Have you found this to be true in your personal experience? Undoubtedly, for many people the answer is a resounding yes. In fact, "who you know" may mean the difference between success and failure. You may have witnessed the quirks and perks of being a member of certain clubs, fraternities, sororities, families, schools or even churches.

However, this should be no surprise since humans are social beings by nature; therefore Organized Effort is a natural part of our behavior. It is a major strategic instinct that accounts for much of our success in surviving the wilds and progressing to our present state. Imagine the survival rate of the human species if we were not bonded together by interdependence. Can one man fight off lions, tigers and bears alone without modern technology?

Unfortunately, most of us also know the disadvantages and disparities that this principle can cause when misused or abused to the detriment of others. However, the scope of this discourse is focused on the benefits of more virtuous application. Dr. Napoleon Hill, author of the Law of Success and Dr. Dennis Kimbro, co-author with Dr. Hill of Think and Grow Rich: A Black Choice documented the experiences of many of the world's greatest achievers concerning the power of harmony, cooperation and mutual support.

At the commission of steel magnate, Andrew Carnegie, Dr. Hill devoted over twenty-five years of his life to develop a philosophy of personal achievement that anyone of average intelligence could learn and apply. According to Dr. Hill, and many others before and since, the action of two or more minds working together, in a spirit of perfect harmony, results in a kind of "Super Mind", more powerful than any of the individual minds. This greater mind is then available to every individual of the group to achieve the common goal.

You have almost certainly observed or even experienced these phenomena to some degree yourself. For instance, those great sports teams in history like the Los Angeles Lakers, Pittsburgh Steelers, or the Tennessee Volunteers Women's Basketball team beyond the competition. Have you ever seen the remarkable ice skating pairs, perform difficult maneuvers beautifully and gracefully?

Synergy, team work, cooperation, networks are manifestation of the natural principle: "The Whole is Greater Than the Sum of its Parts." Think very carefully about this phenomenon and endeavor to make use of it. Learn to recognize and emulate the power underlying all successful teams, groups and partnerships.

Any two individuals may learn to harmonize their mind and organize their efforts to achieve common ends. This is particularly potent for those of opposite gender. You see nature has complimented the design of men and women in more dazzling ways than you may have imagined? But such successful unions must be consciously built up and sustained, thought by thought, step by step. Ask anybody who has maintained a successful relationship over a long period of time.

However, since the power of a network is generated by interconnected parts functioning as a whole; the strength of the whole is relative to the strength of the parts. That is, when every part of a system does it function well, that system will be vibrant and healthy according to its design.

Have you ever seen work groups were one or two people achieve 80% of the results and compared those results to group where more of the people achieve more of the results? The difference between the two can sometimes be very distinctive. Basketball fans may remember the Chicago Bulls stage of development when Michael "Air" Jordan produced 80% of the results. Yet, the Bulls did not win a championship until Scottie Pippin, Horace Grant and John Paxton harmonized with Jordan to contribute more. Then and only then did the Bulls win three consecutive championships!

You see, you are a composition of many parts, a system of integrated systems. Therefore, you are accustomed to speaking of your digestive system, nervous system, circulator system, respiratory system and so on, as separate; yet integral parts of a greater whole. You may even speak of a triune nature in terms of mind, body and soul.

Furthermore, science has long ago identified that symmetry in nature which provides you a right and left hemisphere of your brain; each predominately controlling opposite sides of your body. Correspondingly, awareness is manifested in you as conscious and subconscious; and this is the point at which I invite you to anchor your thought.

Subconscious, by definition is beneath your conscious awareness; it is nature's "Life Support System" in you. It is responsible for the health and operation of every cell, every tissue, every muscle, bone and organ that is the body human. It is the storehouse of all your experiences, the source of your dreams and the workshop of all your intuition. It is the door to all that is divine in you. It is the resting place of all your potential.

Note here that there are two distinct things that you must know about subconscious. First, it is your life support system and as such it is extremely responsive to your needs. For instance, just as it directs the immune system to dispatch white blood cells to attack foreign substances in your blood, it will also drive you to avoid pain and seek pleasure. And if you have any strong, emotionally compelling belief, it will produce the result.

Second, your subconscious is amenable to any suggestion which is successfully impressed upon it. That is it cannot tell the difference between that which you imagine or that which you actually experience. Surely, you have seen the power of hypnosis, whether at a stage show or in a professional hypnotist's office. Individuals after entering a state of trance or sleep, respond in strict accordance with the nature of the suggestion which they received.

In most cases, this is not trickery or quackery, it is well documented, scientific fact supported by the recognition of the nature of subconscious mind. Remember, it is the role of the conscious awareness to distinguish between reality and imagination. In this function, an enlightened conscious is a potent possession.

You see, when the conscious is ignorant of the nature and role of the subconscious, that life is blinded to the most powerful of all of its provisions. This usually leads to significant misuse and abuse of an otherwise priceless asset. Therefore, it is clear that the role and nature of your conscious awareness is to bring the subconscious into consciousness. That is to focus voluntary attention on utilizing the subconscious more effectively and efficiently. Then by virtue of its very nature, your subconscious will respond in the direction of your call.

Remember that great power is generated when two or minds cooperate in spirit of perfect harmony to achieve common goals. By the law of correspondence this holds good for the inside as well as the outside, for the private and the public. Your mind is designed to function as a whole, complete system; even though it is dual in nature.

Reflect on this idea often; make it a habit. Speak to your subconscious with the firm assurance of a perfect partnership. Address it as if you are speaking to a distinct person and resolve to impress upon him/her that your interest are one and the same. Expect perfect cooperation, desire perfect union and believe that you shall receive the benefits of your commands. Diligently search for any information that you can find on the subject and you shall soon find that the information will find you.

You can build perfect harmony between your conscious and subconscious. You can create an interior network focused on your needs. You can generate Diamond, the synergy of conscious and subconscious mind, as the basis of your contribution to external networks. This will amplify your efforts to amazing degrees. You will be pleased with the results.

At the Mouths of Babes

Momma's Alms

Momma: Listen my children and know this truth, the Lord is the love that I give to you, open your hearts and receive his boon. The Lord is the life that I live with you, open your mind and perceive this too. The Lord is the light that I shine for you. Open your eyes to reveal this truth.

Children: Honor and grace to you Momma. Praise and glory to the Lord.

Momma: When the streets are mean and the day is long, hold this thought to keep you strong: Do not haste to waste your time; but keep your mind on the sure incline. Do not give your strength to the foolish my Sons; for they bring nothing and leave you with none. And do not give your strength to vanity my daughters and pearls; for this profits you nothing and misleads the world.

Children: Your works are true and surely correct; but what is our strength that you pay we respect.

Momma: This is your strength and your great stronghold; Love the Lord your God with all you heart, mind and soul. Bless the lamb, praise the light, and know the I Am that is the life. Honor your Father in heaven and Daddy on earth;

for this is the fire that lights the hearth. As for me my children and all that I do, my hope is the knowledge that you know it is for you.

Children: Peace and goodwill to you Momma. Glory and honor to highest.

See It Through

Listen my children for the good and true; for there is a thing that you must do, it sets the lives of those apart who keeps this blessing close to heart:

When your friends are in frolic and it is not time to play, keep your heart from going astray; if you decline and your time they demand, hold your thoughts on the task at hand.

So, when the Anvil you Hammer strikes hold your rhythm and good tight; if your arms get tired and a little slight, carry on all with all your might.

Now as the hours flow and it time to quit strike one more blow and you'll be fit to continue on another day a little further on your way...

Of all the good that you would do, set your mind to see it through; to earn the goal and true reward you must finish my Children, what you start.

So with Courage, Faith and Fortitude, you may say to Life with gratitude, "I thank you for the Attitude to do my best on your greatest quest to the Highest."

In Deep Soil

Children of the Toil anchor your roots in the deep soil of
your Soul and spread your branches to the Light that
unfolds you.

By the might of your back, by the sweat of your brow the
knowledge that you lacked is before you now.

As the wheel turns and the pendulum swings; this truth
you relearn is in the songs you bring.

Listen to Heaven, it has known you a long time; you are
forgiven when your Faith has entwined you.

Open your Heart and incline your Minds; it's your new
start, and the point of the rhyme is the fruit in the line that
there is no other Time like the beautiful, and ever present.
. .

Beyond Freedom

What lies beyond Freedom, O' you children of
the Toil? Chains unseen, Thoughts unclean
bring only poverty and spoil.

Maybe there's a green field in the hills of
Hollywood; but what is the yield when you are
still misunderstood?

Invisible thorns, entwine your Mind;
irresistible scenes incline your demise.

What lies beyond Freedom, O' you Children of
the Sun? Is it Forty Acres and Mule or do you
require something more fun?

Many are the Souls that paved the way with
blood for untold days and nights for you.

Now you can vote. Do you?
Now you can learn. Do you?
Now you can turn your Freedom into . . .

Will You?

African Diamond Mind

Posterity

In a World full of crimes of every kind, True Light in the Labor room continues to shine. In days of many evil ways, Little Souls are singing . . .

"O, leave us a better World, won't you leave us a better World. Your little Boys and Girls need a living World."

Can you see it in the night sky? Their Tears are falling like the Troubled Rain; Little Lives are hoping for a World without so much pain.

Listen to the gentle Winds they are singing to save the Trees, open your Heart and hear these loving pleas . . .

"Save us a better World, O' some of the beautiful Trees; because little Boys and Girls need clean Seas. We believe that you are bigger than your Wars; can we be relieved that you are our ancestors."

In the Womb, before they see any daylight, they're hearing the sound of a World full of strife. We're wearing out the atmosphere and punched a hole in the Ozone; Mary's memory is dying in the streets and Billy's home alone.

When our Hope seems to fail in times of need; the sounds of a new Soul bends our knees in pleading . . .

Save them a World, won't you save them a better World? Our boys and girls need a living World.

Oh won't you open our Hearts, to bring Peace and Harmony. Teach us the sacred Art of Fellowship with all Humanity. Lift out Minds and teach us how to care, for its One LIFE that we all must share.

Save us a better World, oh won't you save our World. All your Children need a living World O', Leave us a better World, won't you leave us a World, we are crying to you to save us a World.

Open your Hearts and listen to the falling rain; these tears are to bring my Light into your MIND again. My living Love is all around you and I'll never leave

So save your World my children, save your World; turn your whole Heart, Mind and Soul to me again. Save you World, my children won't you save your World.

By Bread Alone

With Head and Heart, I do my part to build health and a wealth of Character.

With Hand and Foot, I put my roots in deep soil and bring forth fruit worthy of the ancient toil.

With Mind and Soul, I withhold my strength from the waste that demands a heavy toll.

By whose works have I heard that I do not live by bread alone; but receive my nourishment for Him who made my bones?

By the Light of Truth, and the Glory of His Throne from the time of my youth I am brought to the known . . .

As Sun light to the Tree, and the Rain to the Sea, so is the Work to thee and me.

Ptah-hotep was son of and vizier to King Assa of the Fifth Egyptian Dynasty. The text below was found in Thebes and can be seen today on display in the Louvre. Ptah-hotep himself, who had grown too old and experienced, wanted to pass on to his son the wisdom of his years. The book of *Precepts* he wrote is considered the oldest known book and is designed to teach virtue and excellence.

Horne, Charles F. *The Sacred Books and Early Literature of the East*. New York: Parke, Austin, & Lipscomb, 1917. pp. 62-78.

The Precepts of PTAH-HOTEP

Precepts of the perfect the feudal Lord Ptah-hotep, under the Majesty of the King of the South and North, Assa, living eternally forever.

The perfect, the feudal lord, Ptah-hotep, say is: O God with the two crocodiles, my lord, the progress of age changes into senility. Decay falls upon man and the decline takes the place of youth. A vexation weighs upon him every day; sight fails, the ear becomes deaf; his strength dissolves without ceasing. The mouth is silent, speech fails him; the mind decays, remembering not the day before. The whole body suffers. That which is good becomes evil; taste completely disappears. Old age makes a man altogether miserable; the nose is stopped up, breathing no more from exhaustion. Standing or sitting there is here a condition of...who will cause me to have my authority to speak, that I've made declared to him the words of those who have heard the counsels of former days? And the counsels heard of the gods, who give me authority to declare them? Calls that he be so and that evil be removed from those that are enlightened; send the double...The majesty of this god says: instruct him in the sayings of the former days. It is this which constitutes the merit of the children of the great. All that which makes the sole equal penetrates him who hears it, and that which it says produces satiety.

Beginning of the arrangement of the good sayings, spoken by the noble lord, the divine father, beloved of God, the son of the King, the firstborn of his race, the perfect and feudal lord Ptah-hotep, so as to instruct the ignorant and the knowledge of good sayings. It is profitable for him who hears them, it is lost to him who shall transgress them.

He says to his son: be not arrogant because of that which you know; deal with the ignorant as with the learned; for the barriers of art are not closed, no artist being in possession of the perfection to which he should aspire. But good words are more difficult to find them the emerald, for it is by slaves that this is discovered among the rocks of the pegmatite.

If you find a disputant while he is hot, and if he is superior to you in ability, lowered the hands, bend the back, do not get into a passion with him. As he will not let you destroy his words, it is utterly wrong to interrupt him; that proclaims that you are incapable of keeping yourself calm, when you are contradicted.

If then you have to do with a disputant while he is hot, imitate one who does not stir. You have the advantage over him if you keep silent when he is uttering evil words. "The better of the two is he who is impassive," say the bystanders, and you are right in the opinion of the great.

If you find a disputant while he is hot, do not despise him because you are not of the same opinion. Be that angry against him when he is wrong; away with such a thing. He fights against himself; require him not further to flatter your feelings. Do not amuse yourself with spectacle which you have before you; it is odious, it is mean, it is the part of a despicable soul so to do. As soon as you let yourself be moved by your feelings, combat this desire as a thing that is reproved by the great.

If you have, as leader, to decide on the conduct of a great number of men, seek the most perfect manner of doing so that your own conduct may be without reproach. Justice is great, in variable, and assured; it has not been disturbed since the age of Osiris. To throw obstacles in the way of the laws is to open the way before violence. Shall that which is below gain the upper hand, if the unjust does not attain to the place of justice? Even he who says: I take for myself, of my own free-will; but says not: I take by virtue of my authority. The limitations of justice are in variable; such is the instruction which every man receives from his father.

Inspire not me and with fear, else God will fight against you in the same manner. If anyone asserts that he lives by such means, God will take away the bread from his mouth; if anyone asserts that he enriches himself thereby, God says: I may take these riches to myself. If anyone asserts that he beat others, God will end by reducing him to impotence. Let no one inspire men with fear; this is the will of God. Let no one provide sustenance for them in the lap of peace; it will then be that they will freely give what has been torn from them by terror.

If you are among the persons seated at meat in the house of a greater man than yourself, take that which he gives you, bowing to the ground. Regard that which is placed before you, but point not at it; regard it not frequently; he is a blameworthy person who departs from this rule. Speak not to the great man more than he requires, for one knows not what may be displeasing to him. Speak when he invites you and your worth will be pleasing.

As for the great man who has plenty of means of existence, his conduct is as he himself wishes. He does that which pleases him; if he desires to repose, he realizes his intention. The great man stretching forth his hand does that to which other men do not attain. But as the means of existence are under the will of Ptah, one can not rebel against it.

If you are one of those who bring the messages of one great man to another, conform yourself exactly to that wherewith he has charged you; perform for him the commission as he has enjoined you. Beware of altering in speaking the offensive words which one great person addresses to another; he who perverts the trustfulness of his way, in order to repeat only what produces pleasure in the words of every man, great or small, is a detestable person.

If you are a agriculturist, gather the crops in the field which the great Ptah has given you, fill not your mouth in the house of your neighbors; it is better to make oneself dreaded by one's deeds. As for him who, master of his own way of acting, being all-powerful, seizes the goods of others like a crocodile in the midst even of watchmen, his children are an object of malediction, of scorn, and of hatred on account of it, while his father is grievously distressed, and as for the mother who has borne him, happy is another rather than herself. But a man becomes a god when he is chief of a tribe which has confidence in following him.

If you abase yourself in obeying a superior,

your conduct is entirely good before Ptah. Knowing who you ought to obey and who you ought to command, do not lift up your heart against him. As you know that in him is authority, be respectful toward him as belonging to him. Wealth comes only at Ptah's own good-will, and his caprice only is the law; as for him who ... Ptah, who has created his superiority, turns himself from him and he is overthrown.

Be active during the time of your existence, doing more than is commanded. Do not spoil the time of your activity; he is a blameworthy person who makes a bad use of his moments. Do not lose the daily opportunity of increasing that which your house possesses. Activity produces riches, and riches do not endure when it slackens.

If you are a wise man, bring up a son who shall be pleasing to Ptah. If he conforms his conduct to your way and occupies himself with your affairs as is right, do to him all the good you can; he is your son, a person attached to you whom your own self has begotten. Separate not your heart from him.... But if he conducts himself ill and transgresses your wish, if he rejects all counsel, if his mouth goes according to the evil word, strike him on the mouth in return. Give orders without hesitation to those who do wrong, to him whose temper is turbulent; and he will not deviate from the straight path, and there will be no obstacle to interrupt the way.

If you are employed in the larit, stand or sit rather than walk about. Lay down rules for yourself from the first: not to absent yourself even when weariness overtakes you. Keep an eye on him who enters announcing that what he asks is secret; what is entrusted to you is above appreciation, and all contrary argument is a matter to be rejected. He is a god who penetrates into a place where no relaxation of the rules is made for the privileged.

If you are with people who display for you an extreme affection, saying: "Aspiration of my heart, aspiration of my heart, where there is no remedy! That which is said in your heart, let it be realized by springing up spontaneously. Sovereign master, I give myself to your opinion. Your name is approved without speaking. Your body is full of vigor, your face is above your neighbors." If then you are accustomed to this excess of flattery, and there be an obstacle to you in your desires, then your impulse is to obey your passion. But he who . . . according to his caprice, his soul is . . ., his body is . . . While the man who is master of his soul is superior to those whom Ptah has loaded with his gifts; the man who obeys his passion is under the power of his wife.

Declare your line of conduct without reticence; give your opinion in the council of your lord; while there are people who turn back upon their own words when they speak, so as not to offend him who has put forward a statement, and answer not in this fashion: "He is the great man who will recognize the error of another; and when he shall raise his voice to oppose the other about it he will keep silence after what I have said."

If you are a leader, setting forward your plans according to that which you decide, perform perfect actions which posterity may remember, without letting the words prevail with you which multiply flattery, which excite pride and produce vanity.

If you are a leader of peace, listen to the discourse of the petitioner. Be not abrupt with him; that would trouble him. Say not to him: "You have already recounted this." Indulgence will encourage him to accomplish the object of his coming. As for being abrupt with the complainant because he described what passed when the injury was done, instead of complaining of the injury itself let it not be! The way to obtain a clear explanation is to listen with kindness.

If you desire to excite respect within the house you enter, for example the house of a superior, a friend, or any person of consideration, in short everywhere where you enter, keep yourself from making advances to a woman, for there is nothing good in so doing. There is no prudence in taking part in it, and thousands of men destroy themselves in order to enjoy a moment, brief as a dream, while they gain death, so as to know it. It is a villainous intention, that of a man who thus excites himself; if he goes on to carry it out, his mind abandons him. For as for him who is without repugnance for such an act, there is no good sense at all in him.

If you desire that your conduct should be good and preserved from all evil, keep yourself from every attack of bad humor. It is a fatal malady which leads to discord, and there is no longer any existence for him who gives way to it. For it introduces discord between fathers and mothers, as well as between brothers and sisters; it causes the wife and the husband to hate each other; it contains all kinds of wickedness, it embodies all kinds of wrong. When a man has established his just equilibrium and walks in this path, there where he makes his dwelling, there is no room for bad humor.

Be not of an irritable temper as regards that which happens beside you; grumble not over your own affairs. Be not of an irritable temper in regard to your neighbors; better is a compliment to that which displeases than rudeness. It is wrong to get into a passion with one's neighbors, to be no longer master of one's words. When there is only a little irritation, one creates for oneself an affliction for the time when one will again be cool.

If you are wise, look after your house; love your wife without alloy. Fill her stomach, clothe her back; these are the cares to be bestowed on her person. Caress her, fulfil her desires during the time of her existence; it is a kindness which does honor to its possessor. Be not brutal; tact will influence her better than violence; her . . . behold to what she aspires, at what she aims, what she regards. It is that which fixes her in your house; if you repel her, it is an abyss. Open your arms for her, respond to her arms; call her, display to her your love. Treat your dependents well, in so far as it belongs to you to do so; and it belongs to those whom Ptah has favored. If any one fails in treating his dependents well it is said: "He is a person . . ." As we do not know the events which may happen tomorrow, he is a wise person by whom one is well treated. When there comes the necessity of showing zeal, it will then be the dependents themselves who say: "Come on, come on," if good treatment has not quitted the place; if it has quitted it, the dependents are defaulters.

Do not repeat any extravagance of language; do not listen to it; it is a thing which has escaped from a hasty mouth. If it is repeated, look, without hearing it, toward the earth; say nothing in regard to it. Cause him who speaks to you to know what is just, even him who provokes to injustice; cause that which is just to be done, cause it to triumph. As for that which is hateful according to the law, condemn it by unveiling it.

If you are a wise man, sitting in the council of your lord, direct your thought toward that which is wise. Be silent rather than scatter your words. When you speak, know that which can be brought against you. To speak in the council is an art, and speech is criticized more than any other labor; it is contradiction which puts it to the proof.

If you are powerful, respect knowledge and calmness of language. Command only to direct; to be absolute is to run into evil. Let not your heart be haughty, neither let it be mean. Do not let your orders remain unsaid and cause your answers to penetrate; but speak without heat, assume a serious countenance. As for the vivacity of an ardent heart, temper it; the gentle man penetrates all obstacles. He who agitates himself all the day long has not a good moment; and he who amuses himself all the day long keeps not his fortune. Aim at fullness like pilots; once one is seated another works, and seeks to obey one's orders.

Disturb not a great man; weaken not the attention of him who is occupied. His care is to embrace his task, and he strips his person through the love which he puts into it. That transports men to Ptah, even the love for the work which they accomplish. Compose then your face even in trouble, that peace may be with you, when agitation is with . . .These are the people who succeed in what they desire.

Teach others to render homage to a great man. If you gather the crop for him among men, cause it to return fully to its owner, at whose hands is your subsistence. But the gift of affection is worth more than the provisions with which your back is covered. For that which the great man receives from you will enable your house to live, without speaking of the maintenance you enjoy, which you desire to preserve; it is thereby that he extends a beneficent hand, and that in your home good things are added to good things. Let your love pass into the heart of those who love you;

cause those about you to be loving and obedient.

If you are a son of the guardians deputed to watch over the public tranquility, execute your commission without knowing its meaning, and speak with firmness. Substitute not for that which the instructor has said what you believe to be his intention; the great use words as it suits them. Your part is to transmit rather than to comment upon.

If you are annoyed at a thing, if you are tormented by someone who is acting within his right, get out of his sight, and remember him no more when he has ceased to address you.

If you have become great after having been little, if you have become rich after having been poor, when you are at the head of the city, know how not to take advantage of the fact that you have reached the first rank, harden not your heart because of your elevation; you are become only the administrator, the prefect, of the provisions which belong to Ptah. Put not behind you the neighbor who is like you; be unto him as a companion.

Bend your back before your superior. You are attached to the palace of the king; your house is established in its fortune, and your profits are as is fitting. Yet a man is annoyed at having an authority above himself, and passes the period of life in being vexed thereat. Although that hurts not your . . . Do not plunder the house of your neighbors, seize not by force the goods which are beside you. Exclaim not then against that which you hear, and do not feel humiliated. It is necessary to reflect when one is hindered by it that the pressure of authority is felt also by one's neighbor.

Do not make . . . you know that there are obstacles to the water which comes to its hinder part, and that there is no trickling of that which is in its bosom. Let it not . . . after having corrupted his heart.

If you aim at polished manners, call not him whom you accost. Converse with him especially in such a way as not to annoy him. Enter on a discussion with him only after having left him time to saturate his mind with the subject of the conversation. If he lets his ignorance display itself, and if he gives you all opportunity to disgrace him, treat him with courtesy rather; proceed not to drive him into a corner; do not . . . the word to him; answer not in a crushing manner; crush him not; worry him not; in order that in his turn he may not return to the subject, but depart to the profit of your conversation.

Let your countenance be cheerful during the time of your existence. When we see one departing from the storehouse who has entered in order to bring his share of provision, with his face contracted, it shows that his stomach is empty and that authority is offensive to him. Let not that happen to you; it is . . .

Know those who are faithful to you when you are in low estate. Your merit then is worth more than those who did you honor. His . . ., behold that which a man possesses completely. That is of more importance than his high rank; for this is a matter which passes from one to another. The merit of one's son is advantageous to the father, and that which he really is, is worth more than the remembrance of his father's rank.

Distinguish the superintendent who directs from the workman, for manual labor is little elevated; the inaction of the hands is honorable. If a man is not in the evil way, that which places him there is the want of subordination to authority.

If you take a wife, do not . . . Let her be more contented than any of her fellow-citizens. She will be attached to you doubly, if her chain is pleasant. Do not repel her; grant that which pleases her; it is to her contentment that she appreciates your direction.

If you hear those things which I have said to you, your wisdom will be fully advanced. Although they are the means which are suitable for arriving at the maat, and it is that which makes them precious, their memory would recede from the mouth of men. But thanks to the beauty of their arrangement in rhythm all their words will now be carried without alteration over this earth eternally. That will create a canvass to be embellished, whereof the great will speak, in order to instruct men in its sayings. After having listened to them the pupil will become a master, even he who shall have properly listened to the sayings because he shall have heard them. Let him win success by placing himself in the first rank; that is for him a position perfect and durable, and he has nothing further to desire forever. By knowledge his path is assured, and he is made happy by it on the earth. The wise man is satiated by knowledge; he is a great man through his own merits. His tongue is in accord with his mind; just are his lips when he speaks, his eyes when he gazes, his ears when he hears. The advantage of his son is to do that which is just without deceiving himself. To attend therefore profits the son of him who has attended. To attend is the result of the fact that one has attended. A teachable auditor is formed, because I have attended. Good when he has attended, good when he speaks, he who has attended has profited, and it is profitable to attend to him who has attended. To attend is worth more than anything else, for it produces love, the good thing that is twice good. The son who accepts the instruction of his father will grow old on that account. What Ptah loves is that one should attend; if one attends not, it is abhorrent to Ptah. The heart makes itself its own master when it attends and when it does not attend; but if it attends, then his heart is a beneficent master to a man. In attending to instruction, a man loves what he attends to, and to do that which is prescribed is pleasant. When a son attends to his father, it is a twofold joy for both; when wise things are prescribed to him, the son is gentle toward his master. Attending to him who has attended when such things have been prescribed to him, he engraves upon his heart that which is approved by his father; and the recollection of it is preserved in the mouth of the living who exist upon this earth.

When a son receives the instruction of his father there is no error in all his plans. Train your son to be a teachable man whose wisdom is agreeable to the great. Let him direct his mouth according to that which has been said to him; in the docility of a son is discovered his wisdom. His conduct is perfect while error carries away the unteachable. Tomorrow knowledge will support him, while the ignorant will be destroyed.

As for the man without experience who listens not, he effects nothing whatsoever. He sees knowledge in ignorance, profit in loss; he commits all kinds of error, always accordingly choosing the contrary of what is praiseworthy. He lives on that which is mortal, in this fashion. His food is evil words, whereat he is filled with astonishment. That which the great know to be mortal he lives upon every day, flying from that which would be profitable to him, because of the multitude of errors which present themselves before him every day.

A son who attends is like a follower of Horus; he is happy after having attended. He becomes great, he arrives at dignity, he gives the same lesson to his children. Let none innovate upon the precepts of his father; let the same precepts form his lessons to his children. "Verily," will his children say to him, "to accomplish what you say works marvels."

Cause therefore that to flourish which is just, in order to nourish your children with it. If the teachers allow themselves to be led toward evil principles, verily the people who understand them not will speak accordingly, and that being said to those who are docile they will act accordingly. Then all the world considers them as masters and they inspire confidence in the public; but their glory endures not so long as would please them. Take not away then a word from the ancient teaching, and add not one; put not one thing in place of another; beware of uncovering the rebellious ideas which arise in you; but teach according to the words of the wise. Attend if you wish to dwell in the mouth of those who shall attend to your words, when you have entered upon the office of master, that your words may be upon our lips . . . and that there may be a chair from which to deliver your arguments.

Let your thoughts be abundant, but let your mouth be under restraint, and you shall argue with the great. Put yourself in unison with the ways of your master; cause him to say: "He is my son," so that those who shall hear it shall say "Praise be to her who has borne him to him!" Apply yourself while you speak; speak only of perfect things; and let the great who shall hear you say: "Twice good is that which issues from his mouth!"

Do that which your master bids you. Twice good is the precept of his father, from whom he has issued, from his flesh. What he tells us, let it be fixed in our heart; to satisfy him greatly let us do for him more than he has prescribed. Verily a good son is one of the gifts of Ptah, a son who does even better than he has been told to do. For his master he does what is satisfactory, putting himself with all his heart on the part of right.

So I shall bring it about that your body shall be healthful, that the Pharaoh shall be satisfied with you in all circumstances and that you shall obtain years of life without default.

It has caused me on earth to obtain one hundred and ten years of life, along with the gift of the favor of the Pharaoh among the first of those whom their works have ennobled, satisfying the Pharaoh in a place of dignity.
It is finished, from its beginning to its end, according to that which is found in writing.

---

www.ingramcontent.com/pod-product-compliance
Lightning Source LLC
Chambersburg PA
CBHW071008040426
42443CB00007B/712